The Art of Consultative Selling

Strategies for Lasting Relationships

Linda Thornton

The Art of Consultative Selling

Contents

The Basics of Consultative Selling 5

    The Importance of Relationships in Sales 7

    Key Differences Between Transactional and Consultative Selling 10

The Foundation of Trust in Sales 15

    Techniques for Establishing Rapport 17

    The Role of Active Listening 20

The Art of Asking Questions 25

    Techniques for Needs Assessment 27

    Understanding Pain Points and Goals 30

Value Proposition Development 35

    Communicating Value Effectively 37

    Aligning Solutions with Customer Needs 40

Emotional Intelligence 45

    The Role of Emotional Intelligence in Consultative Selling. 48

    Enhancing Your Emotional Intelligence Skills 51

Strategies for Relationship Maintenance 55

    The Importance of Follow-up 57

The Art of Consultative Selling

    Leveraging Customer Feedback 60

Strategies for Handling Objections 65

    Techniques for Conflict Resolution 67

    Maintaining Professionalism Under Pressure 70

Key Performance Indicators for Relationship Sales 75

    Tools for Tracking Sales Performance............................... 77

    Continuous Improvement and Learning........................... 80

Successful Consultative Selling Examples 85

    Lessons Learned from Failures 88

    Real-world Applications of Techniques 90

Trends Shaping the Sales Landscape 95

    The Impact of Technology on Relationship Sales 98

    Preparing for the Future of Sales 101

About the Author: - Linda Thornton 105

The Art of Consultative Selling

The Art of Consultative Selling

The Basics of Consultative Selling

Consultative selling is a sales approach focused on understanding the client's needs and providing tailored solutions rather than simply pushing a product. At its core, consultative selling emphasizes the importance of building relationships with clients. This technique requires sales professionals to engage in meaningful conversations that uncover the underlying challenges and goals of their clients. By prioritizing the client's perspective, sales professionals can foster trust and establish long-term partnerships, which are essential in today's competitive market.

A key component of consultative selling is the ability to ask the right questions. Sales professionals must cultivate a habit of inquiry, using open-ended questions to delve deeper into the client's situation. This process not only reveals critical information but also demonstrates genuine interest in the client's needs. Effective questioning allows sales professionals to gather insights that can lead to more personalized solutions. Moreover, listening actively to the responses is equally

The Art of Consultative Selling

important, as it helps in building rapport and understanding the emotional drivers behind the client's decisions.

Emotional intelligence plays a significant role in consultative selling. Sales professionals with high emotional intelligence can better recognize and manage their own emotions while also empathizing with their clients. This skill enables them to navigate complex conversations, address concerns, and respond to objections in a constructive manner. By being attuned to the emotional landscape of their clients, sales professionals can tailor their communication strategies and build stronger connections, ultimately leading to more successful outcomes.

In addition to emotional intelligence, consultative selling requires a solid understanding of value-based selling techniques. Sales professionals must articulate the value proposition of their solutions in a way that resonates with the client s specific needs and priorities. This involves not only presenting features and benefits but also demonstrating how the solution addresses the client s pain points and contributes to their overall success. By aligning their offerings with the client s objectives, sales professionals can position themselves as trusted advisors rather than mere vendors.

Finally, successful consultative selling hinges on the commitment to continuous improvement and learning. Sales professionals should regularly seek feedback from clients and react on their interactions to identify areas for growth. This commitment to personal and professional development enhances their ability to adapt to changing client needs and market dynamics. By embracing lifelong learning, sales professionals can renew their consultative selling techniques, strengthen relationships, and ultimately drive better business results for both themselves and their clients.

The Importance of Relationships in Sales

In the landscape of sales, relationships are the cornerstone of success. In consultative selling, the ability to forge and maintain strong relationships with clients can significantly impact outcomes. Sales professionals who prioritize relationship-building not only enhance customer satisfaction but also foster loyalty, which is invaluable in a competitive market. By

The Art of Consultative Selling

establishing trust and rapport, salespeople can better understand their clients' needs and tailor their offerings, accordingly, leading to mutually beneficial outcomes.

The dynamics of relationship sales highlight the importance of emotional intelligence in understanding clients' emotions and motivations. Sales professionals who demonstrate high emotional intelligence can engage with clients on a deeper level, recognizing non-verbal cues and emotional responses. This understanding enables them to navigate conversations more effectively, addressing concerns and reinforcing positive sentiments. As a result, clients feel valued and understood, which enhances their willingness to invest in a long-term partnership with the salesperson.

Value sales techniques emphasize the need to communicate the unique value proposition of a product or service effectively. When sales professionals build strong relationships, they create an environment where clients feel comfortable discussing their challenges and aspirations. This openness allows salespeople to position their solutions as not just products, but as essential tools for achieving the clients' goals. By aligning their offerings with the clients' needs, sales professionals can demonstrate genuine value, making it easier to close deals and secure repeat business.

Consultative selling techniques further reinforce the significance of relationships in sales. This approach requires sales professionals to act as trusted advisors rather than mere vendors. By engaging in active listening and asking insightful questions, salespeople can uncover deeper insights about their clients' businesses. This consultative approach not only strengthens the relationship but also positions the salesperson as a valuable resource, which can lead to increased referrals and expanded opportunities within the client's network.

Ultimately, the importance of relationships in sales cannot be overstated. In a world where transactional interactions are increasingly common, those who invest time and effort into cultivating meaningful connections will stand out. The ability to build trust, demonstrate emotional intelligence, and provide value through consultative techniques will not only enhance individual sales performance but will also contribute to the long-term success of the organization. Sales professionals who embrace the art of relationship building will nd themselves better equipped to navigate the complexities of modern sales environments.

Key Differences Between Transactional and Consultative Selling

Transactional selling focuses on immediate sales and short-term gains, prioritizing the completion of a sale over building a relationship with the customer. In this approach, the salesperson typically emphasizes product features, pricing, and quick solutions. The primary goal is to close the deal as efficiently as possible, often relying on persuasive techniques and promotional offers. This method can be effective in high-volume environments where customers are primarily motivated by price and product availability, such as in retail or commodity sales. However, it often neglects the deeper needs and preferences of the customer, potentially leading to a lack of loyalty and repeat business.

The Art of Consultative Selling

In contrast, consultative selling emphasizes understanding the customer s unique needs and challenges. Sales professionals who adopt this approach engage in meaningful conversations to uncover pain points and aspirations. Rather than pushing a product, the salesperson acts as a trusted advisor, providing tailored solutions that align with the customer's long-term goals. This strategy requires a deep understanding of the customer's industry and the ability to empathize with their situation. By fostering a collaborative dialogue, consultative sellers can create value that extends beyond the immediate transaction, leading to stronger relationships and increased customer loyalty.

One key difference between these two selling styles lies in the salesperson's mindset. Transactional sellers often view customers as a means to an end, while consultative sellers prioritize building rapport and trust. This distinction is critical, as emotional intelligence plays a significant role in the effectiveness of consultative selling. Sales professionals must be adept at recognizing and responding to the emotional cues of their clients. By developing strong interpersonal skills, they can create an environment where customers feel valued and

The Art of Consultative Selling

understood, ultimately enhancing the likelihood of a successful sale and long-term partnership.

Furthermore, the outcomes of each selling approach differ significantly. Transactional selling may lead to quick wins, but it often results in a high churn rate, as customers may not feel a connection to the brand or the salesperson. Conversely, consultative selling fosters loyalty and repeat business, as customers are more likely to return to a seller who has demonstrated genuine care for their needs. This long-term perspective aligns with the principles of relationship selling, where the emphasis is on nurturing connections over time, rather than focusing solely on immediate financial gain.

Finally, the skills required for each approach diverge as well. Transactional selling relies heavily on negotiation tactics, closing strategies, and pressure techniques, which can sometimes backfire if the customer feels manipulated. In contrast, consultative selling demands active listening, empathy, and problem-solving abilities. Sales professionals must be comfortable asking probing questions and engaging in

The Art of Consultative Selling

discussions that may not immediately lead to a sale. By honing these consultative skills, salespeople can transition from a transactional mindset to one that values collaboration and partnership, ultimately leading to more sustainable success in their careers.

The Art of Consultative Selling

The Art of Consultative Selling

The Foundation of Trust in Sales

Trust serves as the cornerstone of effective sales relationships, particularly in the realms of relationship and value selling. It is essential for sales professionals to understand that trust is not merely a byproduct of successful transactions but a fundamental element that underpins every interaction with clients. Establishing trust involves demonstrating reliability, integrity, and a genuine commitment to the client's interests. When clients trust a salesperson, they are more likely to engage openly, share their needs, and ultimately make purchasing decisions based on the value perceived in the relationship.

One of the most effective ways to build trust is by practicing active listening. This allows sales professionals to fully understand their clients' challenges and aspirations. By attentively engaging with clients, salespeople can demonstrate empathy and respect for their concerns, which fosters a deeper connection. Listening goes beyond hearing words; it requires interpreting the emotional cues and underlying needs that clients may not explicitly express. This level of engagement not

The Art of Consultative Selling

only positions the salesperson as a trusted advisor but also enhances the consultative selling process by tailoring solutions that genuinely address client needs.

Transparency is another critical element in establishing trust. Sales professionals should strive to communicate openly about their products, services, and any potential limitations. Clients appreciate honesty, and when salespeople provide clear information about what they can expect, it reduces uncertainty and builds confidence in the relationship. Moreover, being forthright about pricing, potential challenges, and even competitive alternatives shows respect for the client's intelligence and autonomy, further solidifying the trust bond.

Emotional intelligence plays a pivotal role in nurturing trust in sales. Understanding one's own emotions and the emotions of others allows sales professionals to navigate complex interpersonal dynamics effectively. By being attuned to clients' feelings, salespeople can respond appropriately to their concerns, preferences, and motivations. This emotional connection not only enhances rapport but also influences clients' perceptions of the salesperson's credibility. A salesperson who can manage their emotions while empathizing with clients is more likely to inspire trust and foster long-term relationships.

Finally, maintaining trust requires ongoing effort and commitment. Trust is not a one-time accomplishment; it must be nurtured through consistent actions and follow-through. Sales professionals should prioritize building long term relationships over immediate sales, focusing on delivering value and support even after the initial transaction. By checking in with clients, seeking feedback, and being readily available to assist with future needs, salespeople can reinforce the trust established in earlier interactions. This commitment to relationship-building is what ultimately distinguishes successful sales professionals in the competitive landscape of consultative selling.

Techniques for Establishing Rapport

Building rapport is a fundamental component of successful consultative selling. Establishing a strong connection with

The Art of Consultative Selling

clients not only enhances communication but also fosters trust, which is essential for long-term relationships. Sales professionals can employ several techniques to create a solid rapport, starting with active listening. This involves genuinely focusing on what the client is saying, demonstrating attentiveness through non-verbal cues, and summarizing their concerns to ensure understanding. By validating their feelings and showing interest in their needs, sales professionals lay the groundwork for a meaningful relationship.

Another effective technique is mirroring the client's body language and speech patterns. Subtly reflecting their gestures, tone, and pace can create a sense of familiarity and comfort. This approach, rooted in psychological principles, helps clients feel understood and accepted, which can significantly enhance their willingness to engage in open dialogue. However, it is important to do this naturally and avoid overdoing it, as that can come off as insincere or manipulative. When done correctly, mirroring can facilitate a smoother interaction and reinforce the connection between the salesperson and the client.

The Art of Consultative Selling

Empathy plays a crucial role in rapport-building. Sales professionals should strive to understand the emotions and motivations behind a client's needs. By putting themselves in the client's shoes, salespeople can respond more effectively to their concerns and tailor their solutions accordingly. This requires a high level of emotional intelligence, enabling sales professionals to read emotional cues and respond in a way that resonates with the client's feelings. Demonstrating empathy not only helps in addressing immediate concerns but also strengthens the overall relationship, as clients are more likely to return to someone who truly understands their challenges.

Personalizing interactions is another powerful technique for establishing rapport. Taking the time to learn about a client's background, preferences, and interests can significantly enhance the relationship. Sales professionals should utilize tools such as CRM systems to keep track of client details and previous conversations, allowing them to refer back to specific points in future discussions. This personalization shows clients that their business is valued, and that the salesperson is invested in their success, which can lead to increased loyalty and referrals.

Finally, maintaining a positive and approachable demeanor is essential in rapport-building. A friendly attitude, coupled with genuine enthusiasm for helping the client, creates an inviting atmosphere for conversation. Sales professionals should also be mindful of their tone and language, opting for clear and encouraging communication. Positivity can be contagious, inspiring clients to feel more comfortable and open during interactions. By cultivating a warm and supportive environment, sales professionals can effectively establish rapport that not only facilitates immediate sales but also lays the foundation for lasting business relationships.

The Role of Active Listening

Active listening is a fundamental skill in consultative selling that significantly enhances the quality of interactions between sales professionals and their clients. This technique goes beyond merely hearing words; it involves fully engaging with the speaker, understanding their needs, and responding thoughtfully. In the realm of relationship and value sales, where the emphasis is on building trust and delivering tailored solutions, active listening

The Art of Consultative Selling

acts as the cornerstone for establishing meaningful connections. By cultivating this practice, sales professionals can better identify client pain points and motivations, ultimately leading to more effective and impactful sales conversations.

One of the primary benefits of active listening is its role in fostering trust and rapport. When sales professionals demonstrate genuine attention to what clients are saying, they signal that their opinions and concerns are valued. This validation not only helps to build a strong emotional connection but also encourages clients to open up about their challenges and aspirations. In consultative selling, where understanding the client s context is crucial, this deeper level of engagement allows sales professionals to uncover insights that may otherwise remain hidden. Trust, once established, becomes a key factor in maintaining long-term relationships and encouraging repeat business.

Active listening also enhances a sales professional's ability to ask the right questions. By carefully analyzing the information shared by clients, sales professionals can tailor their inquiry to

The Art of Consultative Selling

delve deeper into specific areas of interest or concern. This targeted questioning not only demonstrates a commitment to understanding the client s needs but also positions the salesperson as a knowledgeable consultant rather than just a vendor. Through this process, sales professionals can gather critical information that informs their approach and allows them to present solutions that resonate with the client s unique situation.

Moreover, emotional intelligence plays a vital role in active listening. Sales professionals who are attuned to the emotional undercurrents of a conversation can respond in ways that acknowledge and address clients' feelings. Recognizing non-verbal cues, such as tone of voice and body language, allows sales professionals to adapt their communication style and approach in real-time. This responsiveness is crucial in consultative selling, where understanding the emotional context can lead to more empathetic interactions and stronger relationships. By integrating emotional intelligence with active listening skills, sales professionals can create an environment where clients feel safe to express their thoughts and emotions.

The Art of Consultative Selling

In conclusion, the role of active listening in consultative selling cannot be overstated. It empowers sales professionals to build trust, ask insightful questions, and connect on an emotional level with clients. By mastering this essential skill, sales professionals can significantly improve their effectiveness in relationship and value sales, ultimately leading to stronger client partnerships. As the landscape of sales continues to evolve, those who prioritize active listening will nd themselves at a distinct advantage, equipped to navigate the complexities of client relationships and drive meaningful results.

The Art of Consultative Selling

The Art of Consultative Selling

The Art of Asking Questions

The art of asking questions is a foundational skill in consultative selling that significantly influences the quality of client interactions and outcomes. Sales professionals must understand that the questions posed during a conversation are not merely a means to gather information; they serve as a bridge to deeper understanding and connection. Effective questioning techniques enable salespeople to uncover the true needs and motivations of their clients, allowing for tailored solutions that resonate on a personal level. By mastering this art, sales professionals can cultivate relationships built on trust, empathy, and value.

Open-ended questions are particularly powerful in consultative selling. These questions encourage clients to elaborate on their thoughts and feelings, providing sales professionals with a wealth of information. For example, instead of asking, "Are you satisfied with your current provider?" a more effective open-ended question would be, "What challenges are you currently facing with your provider?" This approach not only invites a more

The Art of Consultative Selling

detailed response but also opens the door for a deeper conversation about the client's needs and desires. By actively listening to these responses, sales professionals can identify pain points and opportunities for value-added solutions.

In addition to open-ended questions, strategic follow-up questions can enhance the dialogue and demonstrate a genuine interest in the client's perspective. These questions help clarify and expand on the initial responses, encouraging clients to think critically about their situations. For instance, after hearing about a specific challenge a client faces, a salesperson might ask, "Can you share more about how that has impacted your team?" This not only shows the salesperson's engagement but also reveals insights that can inform the development of a tailored proposal. The ability to navigate through layers of inquiry fosters a consultative approach that prioritizes the client s needs.

Emotional intelligence plays a critical role in the questioning process. Sales professionals equipped with emotional intelligence can gauge not only what is said but also the emotions behind the words. Understanding non verbal cues and

The Art of Consultative Selling

emotional undertones allows for more empathetic questioning, creating a safe space for clients to express their concerns and aspirations. By being attuned to the emotional landscape of the conversation, sales professionals can ask questions that resonate on a deeper level, thereby strengthening the relationship and enhancing the consultative selling process.

Ultimately, the art of asking questions requires practice, patience, and a willingness to adapt. Sales professionals should continuously review their questioning techniques through role-playing, feedback, and self-reflection. By embracing a mindset of curiosity and openness, they can transform their interactions with clients from mere transactions into meaningful engagements. The ability to ask the right questions at the right time not only drives sales success but also fosters lasting relationships that are built on mutual understanding and shared goals.

Techniques for Needs Assessment

Needs assessment is a crucial process in consultative selling that allows sales professionals to uncover the specific

The Art of Consultative Selling

requirements and motivations of their clients. This process involves a series of techniques that facilitate meaningful conversations, helping salespeople identify not only what the customer needs but also why those needs exist. By employing effective needs assessment techniques, sales professionals can tailor their approaches, create personalized solutions, and ultimately foster strong, lasting relationships with their clients.

One effective technique for needs assessment is active listening. This involves giving full attention to the client, acknowledging their concerns, and reflecting back what they say to confirm understanding. Active listening helps to build rapport and trust, as clients feel heard and valued. Sales professionals can enhance their active listening skills by minimizing distractions during conversations, maintaining eye contact, and using verbal affirmations to encourage clients to share more about their needs. Through this technique, salespeople can gather valuable insights that inform their sales strategies and solutions.

The Art of Consultative Selling

Another technique is the use of open-ended questions. These questions encourage clients to express their thoughts and feelings in greater detail, providing sales professionals with deeper insights into their needs. For instance, instead of asking, "Are you satisfied with your current solution?" a sales professional might ask, "What challenges are you facing with your current solution?" This approach not only reveals specific pain points but also allows clients to articulate their needs in their own words. By fostering a dialogue centered on the client's experiences, sales professionals can uncover underlying issues that may not be immediately apparent.

Incorporating emotional intelligence into the needs assessment process is also vital. Sales professionals should be attuned to the emotions and non-verbal cues of their clients, as these can provide critical context for understanding their needs. By recognizing signs of frustration, enthusiasm, or skepticism, sales professionals can tailor their responses and solutions accordingly. Emotional intelligence allows for a more empathetic approach, enabling salespeople to connect with clients on a personal level and address not only their technical requirements but also their emotional drivers.

Finally, validating and prioritizing identified needs is essential for effective needs assessment. After gathering insights through active listening and open-ended questions, sales professionals should summarize the key points discussed and confirm their understanding with the client. This validation ensures that both parties are aligned on the needs identified. Furthermore, prioritizing these needs helps sales professionals focus on the most critical issues first, allowing them to present tailored solutions that resonate with the client. By systematically addressing the client s needs, sales professionals can enhance their consultative selling approach and create a foundation for long-term relationships.

Understanding Pain Points and Goals

Understanding pain points and goals is fundamental to effective consultative selling. Pain points refer to specific problems or challenges that potential clients face, which can hinder their success or satisfaction. Identifying these pain points allows sales professionals to position their products or services as viable solutions. It requires active listening and thorough questioning to uncover the underlying issues, as clients may not always articulate their struggles directly. By taking the time to understand these challenges, sales professionals can build trust and demonstrate their commitment to genuinely helping clients.

In addition to pain points, it is essential to comprehend the goals that clients aim to achieve. These goals can range from increasing revenue and improving operational efficiency to enhancing customer satisfaction or expanding market reach. By understanding what drives a client's aspirations, sales professionals can tailor their approach to align with these objectives. This alignment not only fosters a stronger connection but also positions the sales professional as a strategic partner rather than just a vendor. Engaging clients in discussions about their goals creates opportunities for collaboration and deeper relationship-building.

Emotional intelligence plays a significant role in understanding clients pain points and goals. Sales professionals who possess high emotional intelligence can read verbal and non-verbal cues, which helps them gauge the client s emotional state and level of

The Art of Consultative Selling

urgency regarding their challenges. This awareness allows for a more empathetic approach, where the salesperson can validate feelings and concerns, creating a safe space for open dialogue. Moreover, emotional intelligence fosters stronger relationships, as clients are more likely to engage with and trust a salesperson who understands their emotional landscape.

Consultative selling techniques emphasize the importance of asking the right questions to gather insightful information about a client s needs. Open-ended questions encourage clients to elaborate on their experiences, providing a clearer picture of their pain points and goals. Techniques such as the SPIN selling method Situation, Problem, Implication, and Need-Payoff can be particularly effective in guiding conversations. By systematically exploring each area, sales professionals can uncover deeper insights that lead to more tailored solutions, ultimately enhancing the value of their offerings.

Ultimately, understanding pain points and goals is not a one-time task but an ongoing process that deepens over time. As relationships develop, clients may face new challenges or shift their objectives, necessitating continual engagement and reassessment. Sales professionals should regularly check in with clients to stay informed about changes in their circumstances and aspirations. By maintaining this dialogue, sales professionals can position themselves as indispensable partners, ensuring long-term success and fostering lasting relationships built on trust and mutual bennet.

The Art of Consultative Selling

Value Proposition Development

Value proposition development is a critical component of consultative selling, serving as the foundation for effective communication between sales professionals and their clients. A well-crafted value proposition clearly articulates the unique benefits and solutions a product or service offers, addressing the specific needs and pain points of potential customers. This process requires a deep understanding of the target audience, including their challenges, motivations, and decision-making criteria. By focusing on these elements, sales professionals can create compelling messages that resonate with clients and foster engagement.

To begin developing a value proposition, sales professionals should conduct thorough market research. This includes analyzing industry trends, customer feedback, and competitor offerings. By identifying gaps in the market and understanding what differentiates their product or service, sales professionals can pinpoint the unique value they bring to the table. This research not only informs the value proposition but also helps in building credibility with clients by showcasing a commitment to understanding their specific needs.

Incorporating emotional intelligence into the value proposition development process enhances its effectiveness. Sales professionals must be attuned to the emotional drivers that influence buyer behavior. This means recognizing and addressing the underlying concerns, fears, and aspirations of potential clients. By aligning the value proposition with these emotional elements, sales professionals can create a more persuasive narrative that speaks directly to the heart of the customer's decision-making process. This empathetic approach not only strengthens rapport but also positions the sales professional as a trusted advisor rather than just a vendor.

Once the value proposition is crafted, it is essential to test and review it based on client feedback and interactions. Engaging in consultative conversations allows sales professionals to gauge how well the value proposition resonates with clients. By asking open-ended questions and actively listening to responses, they can gather insights that highlight areas for improvement. This iterative process not only hones the value proposition but also deepens the relationship with clients, demonstrating a commitment to their success and satisfaction.

Ultimately, a strong value proposition serves as a powerful tool in consultative selling that can significantly impact sales outcomes. It provides a clear framework for communicating the benefits of a product or service while reinforcing the sales professional's role as a problem solver. By continuously developing and adapting their value propositions, sales professionals can foster lasting relationships built on trust, understanding, and mutual value, leading to increased customer loyalty and long-term success.

Communicating Value Effectively

In the realm of consultative selling, communicating value effectively is paramount to establishing trust and fostering long-term relationships with clients. Sales professionals must move beyond simply presenting products or services; they should focus on articulating the unique benefits that resonate with the specific needs and challenges of their clients. This involves a

The Art of Consultative Selling

deep understanding of the client s business, industry trends, and individual pain points. By tailoring conversations to highlight how their offerings create tangible value, sales professionals can differentiate themselves from competitors and position themselves as trusted advisors.

To communicate value, it is crucial for sales professionals to employ active listening skills. This means not only hearing what clients say but also understanding the underlying emotions and motivations that drive their decisions. By asking open-ended questions, salespeople can uncover insights that lead to deeper conversations about the client s objectives. Emotional intelligence plays a critical role in this process, as it allows sales professionals to empathize with clients and respond in ways that demonstrate genuine concern for their success. By building rapport and trust through effective listening, sales professionals can create a foundation for meaningful dialogue about value.

Another key aspect of communicating value is the ability to articulate the return on investment (ROI) that clients can expect from a product or service. This requires sales professionals to be equipped with data and case studies that illustrate past successes and quantify benefits. By presenting compelling evidence of how their solutions have positively impacted similar clients, sales professionals can enhance credibility and make a stronger case for the value they provide. This approach not only helps clients visualize the potential outcomes but also reinforces the idea that the salesperson is invested in their success.

Visual aids and storytelling can also be powerful tools for conveying value. By using graphs, charts, or relatable anecdotes, sales professionals can make complex concepts more accessible and memorable. Storytelling, in particular, allows salespeople to connect on an emotional level, making the value proposition more relatable and impactful. When clients can see themselves in the success stories shared by sales professionals, they are more likely to engage and consider the proposed solutions seriously. This narrative approach can bridge the gap between features and benefits, illustrating how the offering directly addresses the client's needs.

The Art of Consultative Selling

Finally, follow-up communication is essential in the value communication process. After initial discussions, sales professionals should maintain an ongoing dialogue with clients to reinforce the value proposition. This could involve sharing additional resources, providing updates on industry trends, or checking in on the client's progress toward their goals. By consistently demonstrating value throughout the relationship, sales professionals can ensure that clients feel supported and understood. This not only solidifies the relationship but also positions the salesperson as a proactive partner in the client's journey, ultimately leading to greater loyalty and repeat business.

Aligning Solutions with Customer Needs

Aligning solutions with customer needs is a cornerstone of effective consultative selling. Sales professionals must first cultivate a deep understanding of their clients' pain points, desires, and goals. This requires active listening and comprehensive questioning techniques that go beyond surface-level inquiries. By engaging in meaningful conversations, salespeople can gather valuable insights that inform their

The Art of Consultative Selling

approach. This understanding allows them to tailor their solutions, ensuring that what they offer resonates with the specific needs of the customer.

To effectively align solutions with customer needs, sales professionals should employ emotional intelligence. Recognizing and responding to the emotional drivers behind a customer's decision-making process can significantly enhance the relationship. Salespeople who demonstrate empathy and understanding can build trust and rapport, making it easier for clients to express their true needs and concerns. This emotional connection not only facilitates more genuine interactions but also positions the salesperson as a trusted advisor rather than just a vendor.

A consultative selling approach involves presenting solutions that not only meet the immediate needs of the customer but also align with their long-term objectives. By articulating how a product or service can contribute to the customer s broader vision, sales professionals can demonstrate value that goes beyond the transaction. This strategic alignment encourages

The Art of Consultative Selling

deeper engagement and fosters a sense of partnership, where the salesperson is seen as an integral part of the client's success.

Furthermore, successful alignment of solutions requires ongoing communication. After the initial sale, follow-up discussions can help to reassess the customer's evolving needs and ensure that the solutions provided continue to deliver value. This proactive approach not only strengthens the relationship but also opens the door for additional business opportunities. By remaining attuned to the changing landscape of customer needs, sales professionals can adapt their offerings and maintain relevance in a competitive market.

Ultimately, aligning solutions with customer needs is about creating a symbiotic relationship where both parties bennet. Sales professionals who master this skill can transform transactions into lasting partnerships. By focusing on the customer's unique context and leveraging emotional intelligence, they can offer tailored solutions that drive satisfaction and loyalty. This commitment to understanding and

The Art of Consultative Selling

meeting customer needs not only enhances the sales process but also cultivates a reputation for reliability and excellence in the consultative selling arena.

The Art of Consultative Selling

The Art of Consultative Selling

Emotional Intelligence

Emotional intelligence (EI) is a critical component in the toolkit of sales professionals, particularly those engaged in relationship and value-based selling. At its core, emotional intelligence refers to the ability to recognize, understand, and manage one's own emotions while also being attuned to the emotions of others. This skill set enhances interpersonal interactions, enabling sales professionals to build stronger relationships with clients and foster meaningful connections that drive sales success. By honing their emotional intelligence, sales professionals can navigate complex social dynamics and respond effectively to the needs and concerns of their clients.

The concept of emotional intelligence encompasses several key components, including self-awareness, self-regulation, motivation, empathy, and social skills. Self-awareness allows sales professionals to understand their emotional triggers and how their feelings affect their behavior. This understanding is crucial in high-stakes sales situations where emotions can run high. Self-regulation involves managing ones emotions to respond appropriately to various situations, which is particularly important in maintaining professionalism during challenging interactions. Together, these two components lay the foundation for effective communication and relationship-building.

Motivation, another pillar of emotional intelligence, drives sales professionals to pursue goals with energy and persistence. When salespeople are intrinsically motivated, they are more likely to exhibit passion and enthusiasm during client interactions, which can be contagious and inspire clients to engage more deeply with the sales process. Additionally, empathy the ability to perceive and relate to the feelings of others enables sales professionals to understand their clients perspectives and tailor their approaches accordingly. This understanding can lead to more personalized solutions that resonate with clients, ultimately resulting in higher satisfaction and loyalty.

Social skills, the final component of emotional intelligence, are essential for successful consultative selling. These skills involve the ability to communicate effectively, build rapport, and

The Art of Consultative Selling

manage relationships. Sales professionals with strong social skills can navigate difficult conversations, negotiate effectively, and resolve conflicts in a manner that strengthens client relationships rather than undermining them. By employing these skills, sales professionals can create a positive environment in which clients feel valued and understood, paving the way for long-term partnerships.

Incorporating emotional intelligence into sales practices is not merely an enhancement; it is a necessity in today s competitive marketplace. As consumers become increasingly discerning and demand personalized experiences, the ability to connect emotionally with clients has become a differentiator. Sales professionals who invest in developing their emotional intelligence will nd themselves better equipped to engage with clients, understand their needs, and ultimately drive sales success through lasting relationships built on trust and mutual respect. By embracing emotional intelligence, sales professionals can elevate their consultative selling techniques, transforming transactions into meaningful connections that foster loyalty and drive sustained business growth.

The Role of Emotional Intelligence in Consultative Selling

Emotional intelligence (EI) is a critical skill for sales professionals engaged in consultative selling. It encompasses the ability to recognize, understand, and manage ones own emotions while also being attuned to the emotions of others. In a consultative selling context, where building long-term relationships and understanding customer needs are paramount, high emotional intelligence allows sales professionals to connect with clients on a deeper level. This connection fosters trust and rapport, making clients more receptive to discussions about their needs and potential solutions.

Sales professionals with strong emotional intelligence can read verbal and non-verbal cues from their clients. This skill enables them to gauge the emotional state of a client during a conversation, allowing them to adjust their approach accordingly. For instance, if a client appears hesitant or anxious, a sales professional can employ empathy to acknowledge those feelings, thereby creating a safe space for open dialogue. By responding appropriately to these emotional signals, sales professionals can tailor their selling strategies to align with the client s emotional landscape, ultimately guiding them toward informed decision-making.

Furthermore, emotional intelligence enhances a salesperson's ability to handle objections and conflicts. In consultative selling, objections are often rooted in emotional concerns rather than logical ones. Sales professionals equipped with high EI can navigate these situations by addressing the emotional undercurrents at play. Instead of merely countering objections with facts and figures, they can validate the client s feelings, which helps to diffuse tension. This approach not only addresses the immediate concern but also strengthens the relationship by demonstrating that the salesperson genuinely cares about the client s perspective.

Developing emotional intelligence is not an overnight process; it requires ongoing self-reflection and practice. Sales professionals can enhance their EI by seeking feedback from

The Art of Consultative Selling

colleagues and clients, engaging in active listening, and practicing mindfulness. Training sessions focused on emotional intelligence can also be beneficial, providing strategies to recognize and manage emotions effectively. By investing in their emotional intelligence, sales professionals can improve their consultative selling techniques, leading to more engaging conversations and, ultimately, better sales outcomes.

The integration of emotional intelligence into consultative selling practices can significantly impact client satisfaction and loyalty. Clients who feel understood and valued are more likely to remain loyal to a brand and recommend it to others. This loyalty is crucial in relationship and value sales, where long-term connections can lead to increased sales opportunities. By prioritizing emotional intelligence, sales professionals can not only enhance their performance but also create a more positive experience for clients, reinforcing the importance of EI in the art of consultative selling.

The Art of Consultative Selling

Enhancing Your Emotional Intelligence Skills

Enhancing your emotional intelligence skills is crucial for sales professionals who aim to build lasting relationships and drive value through consultative selling techniques. Emotional intelligence (EI) refers to the ability to recognize, understand, and manage ones own emotions, as well as the ability to recognize and influence the emotions of others. In the context of sales, developing these skills can lead to stronger connections with clients, improved communication, and a greater ability to respond to their needs effectively.

One of the key components of emotional intelligence is self-awareness. Sales professionals can enhance their self-awareness by regularly reflecting on their emotional responses in various sales situations. Keeping a journal can be a useful practice, allowing you to document your feelings during interactions with clients, as well as the outcomes of those interactions. By identifying patterns in your emotional responses, you can learn to manage them more effectively, leading to improved interactions and a better understanding of how your emotions impact your sales approach.

The Art of Consultative Selling

Empathy is another critical aspect of emotional intelligence that can significantly influence your success in consultative selling. By actively listening to your clients and trying to understand their perspectives, you can tailor your approach to meet their specific needs. Practicing empathy involves more than just hearing what your clients say; it requires you to engage with their emotions genuinely. Techniques such as mirroring body language and paraphrasing their concerns can help you build rapport and trust, which are essential for fostering long-term relationships.

Additionally, developing emotional regulation skills is vital for maintaining professionalism in challenging sales scenarios. High-pressure situations can trigger strong emotional reactions, which may cloud your judgment or lead to negative interactions with clients. Sales professionals can benefit from techniques such as deep breathing, mindfulness, or positive visualization to manage their emotions effectively. By maintaining composure and responding thoughtfully rather than reactively, you can navigate difficult conversations and keep the focus on providing value to your clients.

The Art of Consultative Selling

Finally, enhancing your emotional intelligence also involves building strong interpersonal skills. This encompasses effective communication, conflict resolution, and collaboration. Training in these areas can help sales professionals engage more effectively with clients and colleagues alike. Participating in workshops, role-playing exercises, or networking events can provide valuable opportunities to practice these skills in real-world scenarios. As you enhance your emotional intelligence, you will nd that your ability to connect with clients and understand their needs will ultimately lead to more successful sales outcomes and enduring relationships.

The Art of Consultative Selling

The Art of Consultative Selling

Strategies for Relationship Maintenance

Effective relationship maintenance is crucial for sales professionals who aim to cultivate long-lasting partnerships with clients. One fundamental strategy is consistent communication. Regular touchpoints, whether through phone calls, emails, or in-person meetings, help maintain a connection and foster trust. It is essential to tailor communication styles to match the preferences of clients, ensuring that interactions feel personal and relevant. This ongoing dialogue allows sales professionals to stay updated on clients needs and challenges, positioning themselves as responsive and attentive partners.

Another key strategy for relationship maintenance is providing value beyond the initial sale. Sales professionals should continuously seek opportunities to offer insights, resources, and support that align with their clients' evolving objectives. This could involve sharing industry trends, offering training sessions, or connecting clients with other valuable contacts within their network. By proactively contributing to clients' success, sales

The Art of Consultative Selling

professionals reinforce their role as trusted advisors, enhancing the overall relationship and encouraging client loyalty.

Emotional intelligence plays a pivotal role in relationship maintenance. Sales professionals must be attuned to their clients' emotions and responses during interactions. By recognizing verbal and non-verbal cues, they can adapt their approach to better meet clients' emotional needs. Empathy is a vital component of emotional intelligence and can help sales professionals navigate challenges or conflicts that may arise. Understanding clients perspectives allows for more effective problem-solving and demonstrates a commitment to their satisfaction and wellbeing.

Another effective strategy is to solicit feedback regularly. Engaging clients in discussions about their experiences, preferences, and areas for improvement not only demonstrates that their opinions are valued but also provides critical insights for enhancing service delivery. This two-way communication fosters a sense of partnership and allows sales professionals to make necessary adjustments to better serve their clients. By acting on feedback, they can show a commitment to continuous improvement, which strengthens the relationship over time.

Lastly, celebrating milestones and successes together can significantly enhance relationship maintenance. Acknowledging important achievements, such as anniversaries of working together, project completions, or client successes, fosters a sense of community and shared objectives. Sending personalized messages, small gifts, or hosting appreciation events can deepen the connection between sales professionals and their clients. By creating memorable experiences and reinforcing a sense of partnership, sales professionals can ensure that their relationships remain strong and mutually beneficial.

The Importance of Follow-up

The importance of follow-up in consultative selling cannot be overstated. In the relationship-focused sales landscape, follow-up serves as a critical bridge between the initial contact and the establishment of a long-term partnership. It is during follow-up that sales professionals can demonstrate their commitment to the client s success and reinforce the value of the solution offered. This process not only helps to solidify the relationship but also facilitates a deeper understanding of the clients evolving needs, enabling sales professionals to tailor their approach more effectively.

Effective follow-up is characterized by its timing and personalization. A well-timed follow-up can remind clients of the conversation they had, and the potential benefits of the solution being offered. It is essential for sales professionals to keep track of client interactions and schedule follow-ups strategically. Personalization is equally important; generic follow-ups can come across as impersonal and may lead clients to feel undervalued. By referencing specific points discussed in previous meetings or acknowledging milestones in the client's business, sales professionals can create a sense of connection that fosters trust and loyalty.

Furthermore, follow-up provides an opportunity to address potential concerns or objections that may have arisen since the last interaction. Clients often require time to process

The Art of Consultative Selling

information and may have questions that they did not think of during the initial meeting. By proactively reaching out, sales professionals can open the lines of communication, allowing clients to voice their thoughts and concerns. This not only positions the salesperson as a trusted advisor but also transforms the follow-up into a collaborative dialogue aimed at finding solutions that meet the client s needs.

In the context of emotional intelligence, follow-up is a key component in building rapport and understanding the client s perspective. Sales professionals who demonstrate empathy and active listening skills during follow-up conversations are more likely to resonate with their clients. By acknowledging the client's feelings and validating their concerns, sales professionals can deepen the emotional connection that is crucial in relationship selling. This emotional engagement helps to create an environment where clients feel understood and valued, making them more receptive to the solutions being offered.

Finally, consistent follow-up can lead to additional opportunities for sales professionals. Satisfied clients are often willing to refer others and may even express interest in additional products or services. By maintaining regular communication, sales professionals can uncover new needs that may arise and position themselves as the go-to resource for the client. This proactive approach not only enhances the relationship but also contributes to the salesperson's overall success, making follow-up an indispensable element of the consultative selling process.

Leveraging Customer Feedback

Customer feedback is an invaluable resource that can significantly enhance the effectiveness of consultative selling. Sales professionals should understand that feedback goes beyond mere satisfaction ratings; it encompasses insights that reveal customer needs, preferences, and pain points. By actively soliciting and analyzing feedback, sales professionals can tailor their approach, ensuring that their solutions align with the specific requirements of their clients. This alignment not only fosters trust but also positions the salesperson as a partner in the client's success, thereby strengthening the relationship.

The Art of Consultative Selling

To effectively leverage customer feedback, sales professionals must adopt a systematic approach to gathering this information. Techniques such as surveys, interviews, and follow-up calls can yield rich insights into customer experiences. It is crucial to ask open-ended questions that encourage clients to express their thoughts candidly. Listening actively to customers responses is equally important; this not only demonstrates respect but also allows sales professionals to identify underlying issues that may not be immediately apparent. By showing genuine interest in customer opinions, sales professionals can reinforce their commitment to meeting client needs.

Once feedback is collected, the next step involves analyzing the data to extract actionable insights. Sales professionals should look for patterns and trends that indicate common challenges or desires among their client base. This analysis can reveal valuable opportunities for upselling or cross-selling, as well as areas for improvement in the sales process itself. By integrating these insights into their sales strategies, professionals can create tailored solutions that address specific customer concerns, thereby enhancing the overall value proposition presented to clients.

The Art of Consultative Selling

In addition to improving sales strategies, leveraging customer feedback can enhance emotional intelligence in sales interactions. Understanding how customers feel about their experiences enables sales professionals to empathize with their clients. This emotional connection can be a powerful tool in consultative selling, as it allows professionals to respond to customer needs in a way that resonates on a personal level. When clients feel understood and valued, they are more likely to engage in open dialogue, providing further insights that can renew the sales approach and solidify the relationship.

Finally, it is essential for sales professionals to communicate back to customers how their feedback has been utilized. By sharing improvements made as a result of customer suggestions, sales professionals not only validate the importance of customer input but also reinforce the idea that they are invested in their clients success. This practice not only enhances customer satisfaction but also builds loyalty, as clients feel they are part of a collaborative process. Ultimately, by leveraging customer feedback effectively, sales professionals

The Art of Consultative Selling

can create a cycle of continuous improvement that benefits both their clients and their own sales performance.

The Art of Consultative Selling

The Art of Consultative Selling

Strategies for Handling Objections

Handling objections effectively is a critical skill for sales professionals, particularly in the realms of relationship and value selling. When a potential client raises an objection, it often indicates a need for further clarification or reassurance. Understanding the root of these objections is essential; they may stem from a lack of information, previous experiences, or fear of change. To navigate these challenges, sales professionals must adopt a proactive approach that emphasizes active listening and empathy, allowing them to address concerns before they escalate.

One effective strategy for handling objections is to use open-ended questions. This technique encourages clients to express their concerns in detail, providing sales professionals with valuable insights into their thought processes. By asking questions such as, Can you tell me more about your concerns regarding this solution? or What specific outcomes are you looking for? sales professionals can uncover underlying issues and tailor their responses accordingly. This approach not only

The Art of Consultative Selling

demonstrates a commitment to understanding the client s perspective but also fosters a collaborative atmosphere where objections are viewed as opportunities for dialogue rather than roadblocks.

Another key strategy involves reframing objections as inquiries. When a client raises an objection, it can be helpful to rephrase it in the form of a question, thereby shifting the conversation from confrontation to exploration. For example, if a client says, I'm not sure this will t within our budget, a sales professional might respond with, What budget constraints are you working with, and how can we adjust our proposal to meet your needs? This technique not only addresses the objection but also invites the client to participate in finding a solution, reinforcing the consultative nature of the sales relationship.

Emotional intelligence plays a vital role in effectively managing objections. Sales professionals who can recognize and respond to the emotional undertones of a conversation are better equipped to address client concerns empathetically. By maintaining a calm and composed demeanor, even in the face of resistance, sales professionals can create a safe space for clients to express their worries. Acknowledging emotions, such as anxiety over a decision, can help to build trust and rapport, making it easier to move past objections and focus on the value the solution brings.

Finally, it is essential to follow up after an objection has been addressed. This step can involve summarizing the key points discussed and reiterating how the proposed solution aligns with the client s needs and values. Additionally, providing supplementary resources or testimonials can reinforce confidence in the solution offered. A thoughtful follow-up not only solidifies the relationship but also demonstrates a commitment to the client s success. By implementing these strategies, sales professionals can transform objections into constructive conversations that ultimately lead to stronger relationships and increased sales success.

Techniques for Conflict Resolution

Conflict resolution is a critical skill for sales professionals, particularly in relationship and value-based selling. Conflicts may arise from misunderstandings, differing expectations, or competitive pressures. Employing effective techniques for conflict resolution can lead to improved relationships and ultimately enhance sales outcomes. Understanding the root causes of conflict and addressing them proactively is essential in maintaining trust and credibility with clients.

One effective technique for resolving conflict is active listening. This involves fully engaging with the other party by paying close attention to their words, tone, and non-verbal cues. By demonstrating genuine interest in their perspective, sales professionals can validate their feelings and concerns, which can de-escalate tension. Active listening not only aids in understanding the conflict but also fosters an environment of open communication where both parties feel heard and respected. This approach is particularly beneficial in consultative selling, where understanding the client's needs and concerns is paramount.

Another valuable technique is the use of I statements. Instead of assigning blame or making accusatory remarks, sales professionals can express their feelings and perspectives using statements that begin with "I." For example, saying "I feel that there may have been a misunderstanding regarding the project timeline" focuses on personal feelings rather than placing blame. This method minimizes defensiveness and encourages a collaborative approach to finding a solution. It is essential in building rapport and maintaining strong relationships, as it emphasizes a shared goal rather than a divisive stance.

Moreover, brainstorming potential solutions collaboratively can be an effective strategy. Engaging the client in a discussion about possible resolutions not only empowers them but also fosters a sense of partnership. By working together to nd a mutually beneficial solution, sales professionals can strengthen their relationships and demonstrate their commitment to the client's success. This technique aligns well with consultative selling principles, where the focus is on creating value for the client rather than merely closing a sale.

Finally, maintaining emotional intelligence throughout the conflict resolution process is vital. Recognizing and managing ones own emotions, as well as empathizing with the emotions of others, can significantly influence the outcome of the interaction. Sales professionals with high emotional intelligence can navigate conflict with greater ease, understanding the emotional dynamics at play. By responding thoughtfully rather than reactively, they can create a more productive dialogue that leads to resolution and strengthens relationships. These techniques collectively form a robust framework for addressing conflict, enhancing the effectiveness of consultative selling practices.

Maintaining Professionalism Under Pressure

In the high-stakes world of sales, maintaining professionalism under pressure is crucial for building and sustaining lasting relationships with clients. Sales professionals often encounter challenging situations that can test their composure, from difficult negotiations to unexpected objections. The ability to remain calm and collected not only reinforces trust with clients but also enhances ones credibility. By developing strategies to manage stress and maintain professionalism, sales

The Art of Consultative Selling

professionals can navigate these pressures effectively, ensuring that their interactions are productive and positive.

One key aspect of maintaining professionalism is the application of emotional intelligence. Understanding and managing ones own emotions, while also being attuned to the emotions of clients, can significantly influence the outcome of a sales conversation. When faced with pressure, a sales professional should practice self-regulation, allowing them to respond thoughtfully rather than react impulsively. This self-awareness can transform tense situations into opportunities for connection, as clients appreciate a calm and empathetic approach even in the midst of challenges.

Active listening is another critical component when under pressure. Clients often express their concerns and needs more vocally during stressful interactions. By focusing on truly hearing what the client is saying, rather than simply preparing a response, sales professionals can uncover valuable insights that may not be immediately apparent. This approach fosters a consultative selling environment where clients feel valued and understood, reinforcing the relationship and encouraging open communication even when discussions become difficult.

Effective communication is essential in maintaining professionalism. Using clear, concise, and respectful language can help defuse tension and clarify misunderstandings. Sales professionals should strive to communicate with confidence while remaining adaptable to the client s tone and emotions. This requires not only verbal skills but also non-verbal cues, such as maintaining eye contact and an open posture, which can convey reassurance and professionalism. By mastering these techniques, sales professionals can create a positive atmosphere that encourages collaboration, even in stressful scenarios.

Finally, developing a mindset of resilience can significantly impact how sales professionals handle pressure. Embracing challenges as opportunities for growth rather than obstacles can shift ones perspective and foster a proactive approach. This resilience can be cultivated through regular reflection on past experiences, seeking feedback, and engaging in ongoing training.

The Art of Consultative Selling

By building a strong foundation of professionalism and emotional intelligence, sales professionals not only enhance their own effectiveness but also contribute to creating a culture of trust and respect within their client relationships, ultimately leading to sustained success in consultative selling.

The Art of Consultative Selling

Key Performance Indicators for Relationship Sales

Key performance indicators (KPIs) are essential metrics that help sales professionals evaluate the effectiveness of their relationship sales strategies. In the context of consultative selling, where the focus is on understanding and addressing the specific needs of clients, KPIs provide valuable insights into performance and areas for improvement. By tracking these indicators, sales professionals can better align their efforts with client expectations and enhance overall sales outcomes.

One of the primary KPIs for relationship sales is the customer retention rate. This metric measures the percentage of customers that continue to do business with a company over a specific period. A high retention rate indicates successful relationship building and client satisfaction, suggesting that the sales professional has effectively addressed the client's needs. By monitoring this KPI, sales teams can identify trends in customer loyalty and make necessary adjustments to their approach, ensuring they maintain strong connections with clients.

Another important KPI is the average deal size, which reflects the revenue generated from each sale. In relationship selling, a larger average deal size may indicate that the sales professional has successfully built trust and demonstrated value to the client, leading to more significant purchases. Tracking this metric allows sales professionals to assess their ability to engage clients in deeper conversations about their needs and how their solutions can provide greater value. It also helps identify opportunities for upselling and cross-selling, enhancing overall sales performance.

Sales cycle length is another critical KPI that can provide insights into the efficiency of the sales process. This metric measures the time it takes to close a sale from the initial contact to final agreement. In consultative selling, shorter sales cycles often indicate that the sales professional has effectively engaged with the client, understood their needs, and presented tailored solutions promptly. Monitoring sales cycle length can help identify bottlenecks in the process and guide sales professionals in revising their strategies to foster quicker decision-making among clients.

Lastly, the number of referrals generated can serve as a vital KPI for relationship sales. Referrals are a strong indicator of client satisfaction and trust, as they reflect clients' willingness to recommend a sales professional to others. A high number of referrals suggests that the sales professional has successfully built lasting relationships and provided exceptional service. Tracking this metric encourages sales professionals to focus on delivering value and nurturing client relationships, ultimately leading to a more sustainable and prosperous sales approach. By leveraging these KPIs, sales professionals can enhance their consultative selling techniques and cultivate emotionally intelligent relationships with clients.

Tools for Tracking Sales Performance

In the dynamic landscape of sales, tracking performance is essential for continuous improvement and long-term success. Sales professionals must leverage various tools that not only measure quantitative metrics but also capture qualitative insights. Customer Relationship Management (CRM) systems are foundational in this regard, enabling sales teams to manage client interactions, track sales activities, and analyze customer data. These platforms often include features for tracking sales pipelines, forecasting revenue, and identifying trends in customer behavior, which are crucial for consultative selling approaches that prioritize understanding client needs.

Another vital tool for sales performance tracking is analytics software. These tools can provide in-depth analysis of sales data, helping professionals identify patterns and correlations that might not be immediately visible. By utilizing analytics, sales teams can better understand which strategies yield the highest conversion rates or which products resonate most with their target audience. Moreover, advanced analytics can offer predictive insights, allowing sales professionals to anticipate customer needs and tailor their pitches, accordingly, thus enhancing the consultative sales process.

The Art of Consultative Selling

Sales performance dashboards are equally valuable, as they offer a visual representation of key performance indicators (KPIs). Dashboards can integrate data from various sources, providing a comprehensive view of individual and team performance. By monitoring metrics such as lead conversion rates, average deal sizes, and sales cycle lengths, sales professionals can quickly identify areas for improvement. These visual tools not only facilitate real-time tracking but also foster accountability within sales teams, as members can see their contributions relative to overall goals.

Feedback mechanisms are another critical tool for tracking sales performance. Regularly soliciting feedback from clients can provide insights that go beyond traditional metrics. By understanding client satisfaction and areas for improvement, sales professionals can adjust their approaches and strategies. This aligns closely with emotional intelligence in sales, as it emphasizes the importance of empathy and active listening. Engaging clients in this way not only strengthens relationships but also creates opportunities for upselling and cross-selling, ultimately driving sales growth.

Finally, mentorship and coaching platforms can enhance the tracking of sales performance by providing professional development opportunities. These tools allow for the monitoring of skills growth and the effectiveness of various sales techniques employed by individuals. By pairing experienced mentors with less experienced sales professionals, organizations can foster an environment of continuous learning, ensuring that the principles of consultative selling and relationship sales are effectively communicated and practiced. This holistic approach to tracking performance not only drives individual success but also cultivates a strong, cohesive sales team.

Continuous Improvement and Learning

In the realm of consultative selling, continuous improvement and learning play a pivotal role in achieving both personal and professional growth. Sales professionals must embrace a mindset that prioritizes ongoing development to adapt to the ever-changing landscape of buyer expectations and market dynamics. This approach not only enhances individual skills but also contributes to building stronger relationships with clients.

The Art of Consultative Selling

By committing to lifelong learning, sales professionals can renew their techniques, develop deeper emotional intelligence, and ultimately deliver greater value to their clients.

One effective strategy for continuous improvement is the practice of self-reflection. Sales professionals should regularly assess their interactions with clients, identifying what worked well and what could be improved. This reflection allows them to gain insights into their selling techniques and emotional responses during conversations. By understanding their strengths and areas for growth, they can tailor their approach in future interactions, ensuring that they consistently meet and exceed client expectations. Additionally, seeking feedback from peers and mentors can provide valuable external perspectives that facilitate personal growth.

Engaging in professional development opportunities is another critical aspect of continuous improvement. Sales professionals should actively pursue training sessions, workshops, and seminars focused on consultative selling and emotional intelligence. These opportunities not only provide new strategies and insights but also foster a collaborative environment where sales professionals can learn from one another. Networking with industry peers can lead to the exchange of best practices and innovative techniques, ultimately enriching each participant's sales approach and enhancing their ability to connect with clients on a deeper level.

Utilizing technology and data analytics can significantly enhance the continuous improvement process. Sales professionals can leverage customer relationship management (CRM) systems and sales analytics tools to gain insights into client behaviors, preferences, and pain points. By analyzing this data, they can identify trends and adapt their strategies accordingly. This data-driven approach allows for more informed decision-making and enables sales professionals to tailor their consultative selling techniques to align with client needs, fostering a sense of trust and partnership.

Lastly, cultivating a culture of continuous improvement within a sales team can amplify individual efforts. Encouraging team members to share successes, challenges, and lessons learned

The Art of Consultative Selling

can create an environment of collective growth. Regular team meetings focused on skill-building and emotional intelligence development can help reinforce the importance of learning and adaptability in consultative selling. By fostering a supportive atmosphere that values improvement, sales professionals can enhance their effectiveness, strengthen client relationships, and ultimately drive better business outcomes.

The Art of Consultative Selling

The Art of Consultative Selling

Successful Consultative Selling Examples

Successful consultative selling hinges on the ability to foster genuine relationships with clients while delivering tailored solutions that address their unique needs. One notable example is a software company that specialized in customer relationship management (CRM) systems. Instead of leading with a hard sales pitch, the sales team took the time to understand the specific challenges faced by prospective clients. They conducted in-depth interviews to uncover pain points, objectives, and operational nuances. This approach enabled them to present a customized solution that not only resolved the immediate issues but also aligned with the client s long term strategic goals, resulting in increased customer satisfaction and loyalty.

Another striking instance occurred within the healthcare industry, where a medical device salesperson adopted consultative techniques to engage with hospital administrators. By focusing on building trust and demonstrating empathy, the

The Art of Consultative Selling

salesperson was able to gather valuable insights regarding budget constraints and procurement processes. Instead of pushing a particular product, they facilitated workshops to educate the administrators about various options available in the market. This collaborative effort led to the hospital adopting a solution that maximized efficiency and improved patient outcomes, showcasing the power of consultative selling in a complex environment.

In the financial services sector, a wealth management advisor exemplified consultative selling by prioritizing emotional intelligence. The advisor recognized that clients often have deeply personal reasons for their financial decisions, ranging from retirement plans to educational funding for children. By adopting active listening techniques and asking open-ended questions, the advisor could navigate sensitive topics and understand the client s life goals. This approach allowed them to create personalized financial plans that resonated emotionally with clients, resulting in stronger relationships and higher retention rates.

The Art of Consultative Selling

A notable example from the real estate market illustrates the importance of consultative selling in a competitive landscape. A real estate agent who focused on consultative techniques spent considerable time understanding the lifestyle preferences and future aspirations of homebuyers. Rather than merely showcasing properties, the agent presented a range of options that t the clients' vision of their ideal life. This strategy not only led to successful transactions but also cultivated a network of referrals, as satisfied clients felt a deeper connection to the agent who truly understood their needs.

Lastly, a B2B marketing agency showcased the effectiveness of consultative selling by implementing a client feedback loop. They invited key clients to participate in quarterly strategy sessions, fostering a collaborative environment where clients could express their evolving needs and concerns. This ongoing dialogue allowed the agency to adapt its services proactively, creating bespoke marketing campaigns that drove measurable results. By treating clients as partners rather than mere customers, the agency solidified its reputation as a trusted advisor, illustrating the long-term benefits of consultative selling in building enduring business relationships.

The Art of Consultative Selling

Lessons Learned from Failures

In the realm of consultative selling, failures can often teach more than successes. Sales professionals frequently encounter situations where deals fall through or clients express dissatisfaction. These moments, while challenging, provide invaluable lessons that can renew techniques and enhance emotional intelligence. Understanding the underlying reasons for these failures allows sales professionals to adapt their strategies, ensuring that future interactions are more productive and aligned with clients' needs.

One common lesson learned from failures is the importance of active listening. In many cases, sales professionals may focus too heavily on their pitches rather than fully understanding the client's concerns or objectives. This misalignment can lead to proposals that do not resonate with the client s needs. By reflecting on past interactions where the outcome was unfavorable, sales professionals can recognize the significance of asking the right questions and genuinely listening to responses. This shift in approach fosters stronger relationships

The Art of Consultative Selling

and positions the salesperson as a trusted advisor rather than just a vendor.

Another critical lesson involves the need for adaptability in sales strategies. The market is constantly evolving, and client needs can change rapidly. Sales professionals who cling to outdated techniques or rigid approaches may nd themselves struggling. Analyzing past failures can reveal patterns that indicate when a strategy is no longer effective. Embracing flexibility in their approach allows sales professionals to pivot quickly, tailoring their solutions to evolving client demands and demonstrating their commitment to providing value.

Moreover, emotional intelligence plays a pivotal role in navigating failures. Sales professionals with high emotional intelligence can better manage their reactions to setbacks, using them as opportunities for growth rather than sources of frustration. By developing self-awareness and empathy, they can gain insights into how clients feel during the sales process. This understanding leads to more meaningful interactions and enhances the salesperson's ability to connect with clients on a deeper level, reinforcing the foundation of consultative selling.

Finally, the experience of failure encourages a culture of continuous improvement. Sales professionals should view setbacks not as endpoints but as steppingstones to greater success. By fostering an environment where feedback is welcomed and lessons are shared, teams can collectively enhance their consultative selling practices. This mindset not only improves individual performance but also strengthens the overall sales strategy, ensuring that the team remains responsive to client needs and competitive in the marketplace. Embracing failure as a teacher ultimately cultivates resilience and a commitment to excellence in relationship and value selling.

Real-world Applications of Techniques

In the realm of consultative selling, the techniques employed by sales professionals have profound real-world applications that significantly enhance relationship-building and value delivery. One of the core principles of consultative selling is understanding the client's needs through active listening and probing questions. This approach not only uncovers the explicit requirements of potential buyers but also reveals underlying motivations and pain points. For instance, a sales professional engaging with a technology rm may discover that their primary concern is not just the price of a software solution but its compatibility with existing systems and the potential for long-term support. By addressing these specifics, the salesperson can position their offering as a tailored solution, thus fostering trust and credibility.

Emotional intelligence plays a critical role in the application of consultative selling techniques. Sales professionals equipped with high emotional intelligence can better navigate the complexities of client interactions. They can read non-verbal cues, gauge the emotional state of their prospects, and adapt their communication style accordingly. For example, during a negotiation, if a salesperson senses that a client is anxious about committing to a long-term contract, they might choose to emphasize flexibility or present alternative options that align with the client s comfort level. This not only alleviates the client s concerns but also strengthens the relationship, demonstrating that the salesperson genuinely cares about the client s well-being and success.

In practical scenarios, relationship sales and value sales techniques often intersect, creating synergistic outcomes. A notable application can be seen in industries where repeat business is crucial, such as in real estate or high-end consumer goods. Sales professionals who prioritize building long-term relationships with clients often employ techniques that emphasize value over price. For instance, a real estate agent might focus on understanding a family's lifestyle needs, presenting properties not merely as transactions but as solutions that enhance their quality of life. This shift in perspective encourages clients to perceive the agent as a trusted advisor rather than just a salesperson, ultimately leading to referrals and repeat business.

Moreover, consultative selling techniques can be effectively applied in training and development programs for sales teams. Organizations that invest in developing the consultative skills of their sales professionals often see improved performance

The Art of Consultative Selling

metrics. For instance, role-playing exercises that simulate client interactions can help sales teams practice active listening, empathy, and strategic questioning. These activities not only build confidence but also reinforce the importance of understanding the client s perspective. By embedding these techniques into the company culture, organizations can create a sales force that is adept at fostering relationships and delivering value, which are essential for sustained success.

Lastly, the integration of technology in consultative selling has transformed how sales professionals engage with clients. Customer relationship management (CRM) systems equipped with analytics tools enable sales teams to track client interactions and preferences over time. This data-driven approach allows sales professionals to personalize their outreach and anticipate client needs. For example, if a client frequently engages with content related to sustainability, a salesperson can tailor their communications to highlight eco-friendly product features. Leveraging technology in this way not only enhances the consultative selling process but also reinforces the salesperson's role as a knowledgeable partner,

The Art of Consultative Selling

ultimately leading to deeper connections and increased sales effectiveness.

The Art of Consultative Selling

Trends Shaping the Sales Landscape

The sales landscape is evolving rapidly, influenced by a multitude of factors that shape how professionals engage with clients. One significant trend is the increasing emphasis on relationship building over transactional selling. In an environment where customers are bombarded with options, sales professionals are finding that nurturing long-term relationships can lead to increased loyalty and repeat business. This shift requires a deeper understanding of the client's needs and motivations, moving beyond mere product features to a more comprehensive approach that integrates consultative selling techniques.

Another trend shaping the sales landscape is the rise of value-based selling. Sales professionals are now expected to articulate the unique value proposition of their offerings in a way that resonates with the specific challenges their clients face. This requires not only a thorough understanding of the product but also an acute awareness of the market dynamics and the client's business objectives. By aligning their solutions with the client's

The Art of Consultative Selling

goals, sales professionals can create a compelling narrative that highlights how their products or services can drive tangible results, thereby differentiating themselves in a crowded marketplace.

The integration of technology into the sales process is another critical trend. With the advent of Customer Relationship Management (CRM) systems, data analytics, and artificial intelligence, sales professionals have more tools than ever at their disposal to understand customer behavior and preferences. Leveraging these technologies allows for more personalized interactions and informed decision-making. As a result, sales strategies are becoming increasingly data-driven, enabling professionals to anticipate client needs and respond proactively, which enhances the consultative selling approach.

Emotional intelligence (EI) has emerged as a vital competency for sales professionals in this changing landscape. Understanding and managing one's own emotions, as well as empathizing with clients, can significantly influence the sales process. High EI allows professionals to connect on a deeper

The Art of Consultative Selling

level, fostering trust and rapport. This is particularly important in consultative selling, where the focus is on collaboration and understanding rather than pushing a product. Sales professionals who cultivate their emotional intelligence can better navigate complex interactions, leading to more successful outcomes.

Finally, the growing importance of sustainability and corporate social responsibility is reshaping buyer expectations. Clients are increasingly looking for partners who share their values and demonstrate a commitment to ethical practices. Sales professionals must be prepared to engage in conversations about sustainability and how their offerings align with these principles. This trend not only affects the products being sold but also the way sales professionals position themselves as trusted advisors. By integrating these values into their sales strategy, professionals can enhance their credibility and strengthen their relationships with clients, ultimately driving sales success in a conscientious marketplace.

The Impact of Technology on Relationship Sales

The integration of technology into the sales landscape has profoundly transformed relationship sales. The traditional approach, which relied heavily on face-to-face interactions and personal rapport-building, has evolved with the advent of tools such as Customer Relationship Management (CRM) systems, social media platforms, and data analytics. These technologies enable sales professionals to gather and analyze vast amounts of customer data, allowing for more personalized and targeted sales strategies. As a result, sales professionals can now develop a deeper understanding of their clients' needs, preferences, and behaviors, ultimately fostering stronger relationships and enhancing the consultative selling process.

One of the most significant impacts of technology on relationship sales is the shift toward a more data-driven approach. Sales professionals can leverage data analytics to identify trends and patterns in customer behavior, which can inform their sales strategies. By utilizing insights from CRM systems, sales teams can track interactions, follow up on leads, and tailor their messaging to resonate with individual clients.

The Art of Consultative Selling

This level of personalization not only improves the effectiveness of sales pitches but also demonstrates a commitment to understanding the client's unique challenges, thereby reinforcing trust and credibility in the salesperson-client relationship.

Furthermore, technology has expanded the channels through which sales professionals can engage with clients. Social media platforms offer new opportunities for relationship building, allowing sales professionals to interact with clients in real time and share valuable content that addresses their interests and concerns. By participating in online conversations and providing thought leadership, sales professionals can position themselves as trusted advisors rather than mere salespeople. This shift aligns perfectly with the principles of consultative selling, where the focus is on providing value and solutions to clients rather than pushing a product.

Emotional intelligence plays a crucial role in the technology-driven sales environment. While technology facilitates data collection and communication, the human aspect of sales remains paramount. Sales professionals must harness emotional intelligence to interpret the data they gather and engage with clients meaningfully. Understanding clients' emotional triggers and motivations allows sales professionals to navigate conversations more effectively and respond to their needs with empathy. This combination of emotional intelligence and technological tools enables sales professionals to create authentic connections, which are essential for long-term relationship building.

In conclusion, the impact of technology on relationship sales has been transformative, providing sales professionals with powerful tools to enhance their strategies. The ability to analyze data, engage through various channels, and apply emotional intelligence enables sales professionals to build deeper relationships with clients. As the sales landscape continues to evolve, those who embrace technology while maintaining a focus on human connection will be best positioned to succeed in consultative selling. The future of relationship sales lies in striking the right balance between leveraging technology and nurturing the emotional bonds that ultimately drive business success.

The Art of Consultative Selling

Preparing for the Future of Sales

In the rapidly evolving landscape of sales, preparing for the future requires sales professionals to adapt their strategies and hone their skills continuously. The rise of technology and changes in consumer behavior have shifted the dynamics of the sales process. To thrive in this environment, sales professionals must embrace consultative selling techniques that prioritize building relationships over mere transactions. This approach not only enhances customer satisfaction but also fosters loyalty, making it essential for long-term success in sales.

To navigate the future of sales effectively, professionals should integrate emotional intelligence into their skill set. Understanding and managing ones own emotions, as well as empathizing with customers, can significantly impact the sales process. Emotional intelligence enables sales professionals to connect with clients on a deeper level, identifying their needs and motivations. By fostering genuine connections, professionals can position themselves as trusted advisors, guiding clients through their purchasing decisions with empathy and insight.

The Art of Consultative Selling

The importance of technology in sales cannot be understated. As digital tools and platforms become more prevalent, sales professionals must learn to leverage data analytics and customer relationship management (CRM) systems to enhance their consultative selling strategies. These tools provide invaluable insights into customer behavior, preferences, and demographics, allowing sales professionals to tailor their approaches. By utilizing technology effectively, they can create personalized experiences that resonate with clients, thereby reinforcing the value of the relationship.

Additionally, continuous learning and professional development are crucial for staying ahead in the sales domain. Attending workshops, webinars, and training sessions focused on evolving sales techniques and emotional intelligence can provide sales professionals with fresh perspectives and innovative strategies. Engaging with peers and industry leaders can also offer insights into best practices and emerging trends. By committing to lifelong learning, sales professionals can position themselves as knowledgeable and adaptable, ready to meet the challenges of the future head-on.

Finally, cultivating a mindset focused on value creation will be essential for sales professionals in the coming years. Clients are increasingly seeking solutions that address their specific pain points rather than generic products. By adopting a consultative approach that emphasizes understanding client needs and delivering tailored solutions, sales professionals can differentiate themselves in a competitive market. This value-oriented mindset will not only enhance client relationships but also drive sales success, ensuring that professionals are well-prepared for the future of sales.

The Art of Consultative Selling

About the Author:
- Linda Thornton

Linda Thornton is a distinguished professor of Business Administration at University of North Carolina, where she has been shaping the minds of future business leaders for over two decades. Her expertise in sales strategy and relationship management is unmatched, making her a sought-after speaker at global conferences. In her groundbreaking book, The Art of Consultative Selling: Strategies for Lasting Relationships, Dr. Thornton combines her extensive research and real-world experience to provide actionable insights for building enduring client relationships. Passionate about education and mentorship, she dedicates her time to guiding young

The Art of Consultative Selling

professionals and exploring the nuances of effective communication and negotiation in the business world.

www.ingramcontent.com/pod-product-compliance
Lightning Source LLC
Chambersburg PA
CBHW070155230526
45471CB00002B/673